Bugs in My Backyard

I See Butterflies

By Julia Jaske

 I see a butterfly.

I see a red butterfly.

4 I see a blue butterfly.

I see an orange butterfly.

 I see a yellow butterfly.

I see a butterfly flying.

8 I see a butterfly smelling.

I see a butterfly relaxing.

I see a butterfly climbing.

I see a butterfly drinking.

I see a butterfly stretching.

I see a butterfly saying hello!

Word List

butterfly	relaxing
red	climbing
blue	drinking
orange	stretching
yellow	saying
flying	hello
smelling	

I see a butterfly.

I see a red butterfly.

I see a blue butterfly.

I see an orange butterfly.

I see a yellow butterfly.

I see a butterfly flying.

I see a butterfly smelling.

I see a butterfly relaxing.

I see a butterfly climbing.

I see a butterfly drinking.

I see a butterfly stretching.

I see a butterfly saying hello!

CHERRY BLOSSOM PRESS

Published in the United States of America by Cherry Lake Publishing Group
Ann Arbor, Michigan
www.cherrylakepublishing.com

Book Designer: Melinda Millward

Photo Credits: ©Candy_Plus/Shutterstock.com, front cover, 1; ©Butterfly Hunter/Shutterstock.com, back cover, 14; ©Shubhrojyoti/Shutterstock.com, 2; ©mexrix/Shutterstock.com, 3; ©ChameleonsEye/Shutterstock.com, 4; ©Christopher PB/Shutterstock.com, 5; ©MindStorm/Shutterstock.com, 6; ©suns07butterfly/Shutterstock.com, 7; ©Stella Photography/Shutterstock.com, 8; ©CHAINFOTO24/Shutterstock.com, 9; ©pimchawee/Shutterstock.com, 10; ©Dave Montreuil/Shutterstock.com, 11; ©Georgi Baird/Shutterstock.com, 12; ©KRIACHKO OLESKSII/Shutterstock.com, 13

Cherry Blossom Press is an imprint of Cherry Lake Publishing Group.

Library of Congress Cataloging-in-Publication Data

Names: Jaske, Julia, author.
Title: I see butterflies / by Julia Jaske.
Description: Ann Arbor, Michigan : Cherry Lake Publishing, 2022. | Series: Bugs in my backyard |
    Audience: Grades K-1
Identifiers: LCCN 2021036283 (print) | LCCN 2021036284 (ebook) | ISBN 9781534198883
    (paperback) | ISBN 9781668905784 (ebook) | ISBN 9781668901465 (pdf)
Subjects: LCSH: Butterflies—Juvenile literature.
Classification: LCC QL544.2 .J37 2022 (print) | LCC QL544.2 (ebook) | DDC 595.78/9—dc23
LC record available at https://lccn.loc.gov/2021036283
LC ebook record available at https://lccn.loc.gov/2021036284

Cherry Lake Publishing Group would like to acknowledge the work of the Partnership for 21st Century Learning, a Network of Battelle for Kids. Please visit http://www.battelleforkids.org/networks/p21 for more information.

Printed in the United States of America
Corporate Graphics